And Baby Makes Three

Wise and Witty Observations on the Joys of Parenthood

MAXINE REED

CB
CONTEMPORARY BOOKS
A TRIBUNE NEW MEDIA COMPANY

Library of Congress Cataloging-in-Publication Data

Reed, Maxine.
And baby makes three : wise and witty observations on the joys of parenthood / Maxine Reed.
p. cm.
ISBN 0-8092-3496-3
1. Parenting—Quotations, maxims, etc. 2. Parenthood—Quotations, maxims, etc. 3. Children—Quotations, maxims, etc. I. Title.
PN6084.C48R44 1995
649'.1—dc20 94-47554
CIP

Published by Contemporary Books, Inc.
Two Prudential Plaza, Chicago, Illinois 60601-6790
Manufactured in the United States of America
International Standard Book Number: 0-8092-3496-3
10 9 8 7 6 5 4 3 2 1

You may have tangible wealth untold;
Caskets of jewels and coffers of gold.
Richer than I you can never be—
I had a mother who read to me.

STRICKLAND GILLILAN

Acknowledgments

The editor would like to thank Bertha, Nancy, and Bob for their help.

Making the decision to have a child—it's momentous. It is to decide forever to have your heart go walking around outside your body.

ELIZABETH STONE

Having a child helps you get your priorities straight. You know that you'll never waste a prayer on anything frivolous again.

ALICE KAHN

Tending gardens and raising children are testimony to one's faith in the future.

NANCY MCCORD

A happy childhood can't be cured. Mine'll hang around my neck like a rainbow.

HORTENSE CALISHER

Family jokes, though rightly cursed by strangers, are the bond that keeps most families alive.

STELLA BENSON

The more people have studied different methods of bringing up children the more they have come to the conclusion that what good mothers and fathers instinctively feel like doing for their babies is the best after all.

DR. BENJAMIN SPOCK

If the new American father feels bewildered and even defeated, let him take comfort from the fact that whatever he does in any fathering situation has a 50 percent chance of being right.

BILL COSBY

Twins: Womb-mates.

KAY FRANCIS

You have the right to make mistakes in bringing up your own children: Blunder bravely! Go ahead and make your mistakes, but believe more bravely that, on the whole, you are doing a good job of raising your children.

FITZHUGH DODSON

The smile that flickers on baby's lips when he sleeps—does anybody know where it was born? Yes, there is a rumor that a young pale beam of a crescent moon touched the edge of a vanishing autumn cloud, and there the smile was first born in the dream of a dew-washed morning.

RABINDRANATH TAGORE

When the first baby laughed for the first time, the laugh broke into a thousand pieces and they all went skipping about, and that was the beginning of fairies.

SIR J. M. BARRIE

Youth smiles without any reason. It is one of its chiefest charms.

OSCAR WILDE

Babies are such a nice way to start people.

DON HEROLD

A babe in a house is a well-spring of pleasure.

MARTIN F. TUPPER

How lovely he appears! his little cheeks
In their pure incarnation, vying with
The rose leaves strewn beneath them.
And his lips, too,
How beautifully parted! No; you shall not
Kiss him: at least not now; he will wake soon—
His hour of midday rest is nearly over.

LORD BYRON

The hair she means to have is gold,
Her eyes are blue, she's twelve weeks old.

FREDERICK LOCKER-LAMPSON

A little child born yesterday,
A thing on mother's milk and kisses fed.

HOMER

What has she got in that little brown head?
Wonderful thoughts which can never be said.

A. A. MILNE

If only we could know what was going on in a baby's mind while observing him in action we could certainly understand everything there is to psychology.

JEAN PIAGET

What is the little one thinking about?
Very wonderful things, no doubt;
  Unwritten history!
  Unfathomed mystery!
Yet he laughs and cries, and eats and drinks,
And chuckles and crows, and nods and winks,
As if his head were as full of kinks
And curious riddles as any sphinx!

J. G. HOLLAND

Raising children is like making biscuits: it is as easy to raise a big batch as one, while you have your hands in the dough.

E. W. HOWE

There is two things in this life for which we are never fully prepared, and that is—twins.

JOSH BILLINGS

When people inquire I always just state,
"I have four nice children, and hope to have eight."

ALINE KILMER

As a father of two there is a respectful question which
I wish to ask of fathers of five:
How do you happen to be still alive?

OGDEN NASH

My child looked at me and I looked back at him in the delivery room, and I realized that out of a sea of infinite possibilities it had come down to this: a specific person, born on the hottest day of the year, conceived on a Christmas Eve, made by his father and me miraculously from scratch.

ANNA QUINDLEN

There came to port last Sunday night
The queerest little craft,
Without an inch of rigging on;
I looked and looked—and laughed.
It seemed so curious that she
Should cross the unknown water,
And moor herself within my room—
My daughter! O my daughter!

G. W. CABLE

Babies are bits of stardust blown from the hand of God. Lucky the woman who knows the pangs of birth, for she has held a star.

LARRY BARRETTO

Yes, having a child is surely the most beautifully irrational act that two people in love can commit.

BILL COSBY

Still as my horizon grew,
Larger grew my riches too;
All the world I saw or knew
Seemed a complex Chinese toy,
Fashioned for a barefoot boy!

JOHN GREENLEAF WHITTIER

Boys do not grow up gradually. They move forward in spurts like the hands of clocks in railway stations.

CYRIL CONNOLLY

A baby hires and enslaves you.

PROVERB

A boy's will is the wind's will,
And the thoughts of youth are long, long thoughts.

HENRY WADSWORTH LONGFELLOW

A boy is an appetite with a skin pulled over it.

ANONYMOUS

Of all the things that I would rather,
It is to be my daughter's father.

OGDEN NASH

What are little girls made of?
Sugar and spice, and everything nice;
That's what little girls are made of.

ANONYMOUS

Children are like puppies: you have to keep them near you and look after them if you want to have their affection.

ANNA MAGNANI

The world has no such flower in any land,
And no such pearl in any gulf the sea,
As any babe on any mother's knee.

ALGERNON SWINBURNE

He never cares to wander from his own fireside,
  He never cares to wander or to roam.
With his baby on his knee,
He's as happy as can be,
  For there's no place like home, sweet home.

FELIX MCGLENNON

What a difference it makes to come home to a child!

MARGARET FULLER

The family is one of nature's masterpieces.

GEORGE SANTAYANA

The God to whom little boys say their prayers has a face very like their mother's.

SIR J. M. BARRIE

James James
Morrison Morrison
Weatherby George Dupree
Took great
Care of his Mother,
Though he was only three.

A. A. MILNE

I must have been a chronically suspicious small boy, for I remember thinking to myself that Father needed a great deal of watching.

CLARENCE DAY

Between the dark and the daylight,
  When the night is beginning to lower,
Comes a pause in the day's occupations,
  That is known as the Children's Hour.

HENRY WADSWORTH LONGFELLOW

Binker—what I call him—is a secret of my own,
And Binker is the reason why I never feel alone.
Playing in the nursery, sitting on the stair,
Whatever I am busy at, Binker will be there.

A. A. MILNE

At evening when the lamp is lit,
Around the fire my parents sit;
They sit at home and talk and sing,
And do not play at anything.

ROBERT LOUIS STEVENSON

A child is the root of the heart.

CAROLINA MARIA DE JESUS

Golf . . . is a trifling thing beside the privilege of taking a small son to the zoo and letting him see his first lion, his first tiger, and, best of all, his first elephant. Probably he will think that they are part of your own handiwork turned out for his pleasure.

HEYWOOD BROUN

I would rather see one of my children's faces kindle at the sight of the quay at Calais than be offered the chance of exploring by myself the palaces of Peking.

J. B. PRIESTLEY

We find delight in the beauty and happiness of children that makes the heart too big for the body.

RALPH WALDO EMERSON

Many an infant that screams like a calliope
Could be soothed by a little attention to its diope.

OGDEN NASH

How to fold a diaper depends on the size of the baby and the diaper.

DR. BENJAMIN SPOCK

The baby wakes up in the wee wee hours of the morning.

ROBERT ROBBINS

Any mother with half a skull knows that when Daddy's little boy becomes Mommy's little boy, the kid is so wet he's treading water!

ERMA BOMBECK

The most important thing a father can do for his children is to love their mother.

THEODORE M. HESBURGH

Gradually I came to know where I was, and I tried to express my wants to those who could gratify them, yet could not, because my wants were inside me, and they were outside, nor had they any power of getting into my soul. And so I made movements and sounds, signs like my wants, the few I could, the best I could; for they were not really like my meaning. And when I was not obeyed, because people did not understand me, or because they would not do me harm, I was angry . . . and I avenged myself on them by tears.

ST. AUGUSTINE

Here we have a baby. It is composed of a bald head and a pair of lungs.

EUGENE FIELD

In the little world in which children have their existence, whosoever brings them up, there is nothing so finely perceived and so finely felt, as injustice.

CHARLES DICKENS

No music is so pleasant to my ears as that word—father. Zoroaster tells us that children are a bridge joining this earth to a heavenly paradise, filled with fresh springs and blooming gardens. Blessed indeed is the man who hears many gentle voices call him father!

LYDIA M. CHILD

He [Dad] took out his memorandum book and solemnly wrote: "Don't forget to have six boys and six girls."

FRANK B. GILBRETH, JR., AND ERNESTINE GILBRETH CAREY

His little children, climbing for a kiss,
Welcome their father's late return at night.

VERGIL

A mother is not a person to lean on but a person to make leaning unnecessary.

DOROTHY CANFIELD FISHER

Women know
The way to rear up children (to be just);
They know a simple, merry tender knack
Of tying sashes, fitting baby-shoes,
And stringing pretty words that make no sense,
And kissing full sense into empty words;
Which things are corals to cut life upon,
Although such trifles.

ELIZABETH BARRETT BROWNING

Some are kissing mothers and some are scolding mothers, but it is love just the same, and most mothers kiss and scold together.

PEARL BUCK

When I am grown to man's estate
I shall be very proud and great,
And tell the other girls and boys
Not to meddle with my toys.

ROBERT LOUIS STEVENSON

When we look at actual children, no matter how they are raised, we notice immediately that little girls are in fact smaller versions of real human beings, whereas little boys are Pod People from the Planet Destructo.

DAVE BARRY

Siblings: Children of the same parents, each of whom is perfectly normal until they get together.

SAM LEVENSON

There is no end to the violations committed by children on children, quietly talking alone.

ELIZABETH BOWEN

Childhood is like a butterfly intent on burning its white wings in the flames of youth.

ALOYSIUS BERTRAND

Infancy isn't what it is cracked up to be. Children, not knowing that they are having an easy time, have a good many hard times. Growing and learning and obeying the rules of their elders, or fighting against them, are not easy things to do.

DON MARQUIS

The young are permanently in a state resembling intoxication; for youth is sweet and they are growing.

ARISTOTLE

Children are remarkable for their intelligence and ardor, for their curiosity, their intolerance of shams, the clarity and ruthlessness of their vision.

ALDOUS HUXLEY

Small children don't let you sleep; big children don't let you rest.

PROVERB

The lack of sleep you get with a child in your bed is of a higher quality than the lack of sleep you get in the child's.

BILL COSBY

Parenthood: That state of being better chaperoned than you were before marriage.

MARCELENE COX

Children who drop in at night are a means of birth control that is one hundred percent effective.

BILL COSBY

Don't bother discussing sex with small children. They rarely have anything to add.

FRAN LEBOWITZ

Among the three or four million cradles now rocking in the land are some which this nation would preserve for ages as sacred things, if we could know which ones they are.

MARK TWAIN

The child with his sweet pranks the fool of his senses, commanded by every sight and sound, without any power to compare and rank his sensations, abandoned to a whistle or a painted chip, to a lead dragoon or a gingerbread-dog, individualizing everything, generalizing nothing, delighted with every new thing, lies down at night overpowered by the fatigue which this day of continual pretty madness has incurred. But Nature has answered her purpose with the curly, dimpled lunatic.

RALPH WALDO EMERSON

No animal is so inexhaustible as an excited infant.

AMY LESLIE

So for the mother's sake the child was dear,
And dearer was the mother for the child.

SAMUEL COLERIDGE

Sweetest li'l feller, everybody knows;
Dunno what to call him, but he's mighty lak' a rose.

FRANK L. STANTON

A baby overwhelms us with its lovableness; even its smell stirs us more deeply than the smell of pine or baking bread. What is overpowering is simply the fact that a baby is life. It is also a mess, but such an appealing one that we look past the mess to the jewel underneath.

BILL COSBY

The best smell is bread, the best savour salt, the best love that of children.

PROVERB

Of course, people who spend more than six minutes trying to discipline children learn that consistency and logic are never a part of things.

BILL COSBY

There's nothing wrong with a child's behavior that trying to reason with him won't aggravate.

SAM LEVENSON

Reasoning with a child is fine, if you can reach the child's reason without destroying your own.

JOHN MASON BROWN

Stop yelling. If you want to ask me something, come here.
STOP YELLING. IF YOU WANT TO ASK ME SOMETHING, COME HERE.

DELIA EPHRON

Never threaten a child with a visit to the dentist.

JANE E. BRODY

Level with your child by being honest. Nobody spots a phony quicker than a child.

MARY MACCRACKEN

Children are forced to live very rapidly in order to live at all. They are given only a few years in which to learn hundreds of thousands of things about life and the planet and themselves.

PHYLLIS MCGINLEY

The mother's heart is the child's schoolroom.

HENRY WARD BEECHER

Whatever you would have your children become, strive to exhibit in your own lives and conversation.

LYDIA H. SIGOURNEY

Parents are Patterns.

THOMAS FULLER

The situation of our youth is not mysterious. Children have never been very good at listening to their elders, but they have never failed to imitate them. They must, they have no other models.

JAMES BALDWIN

Parents repeat their lives in their offspring; and their esteem for them is so great that they feel their sufferings and taste their enjoyments as much as if they were their own.

RAY PALMER

Child! do not throw this book about;
Refrain from the unholy pleasure
Of cutting all the pictures out!
Preserve it as your chiefest treasure.

HILAIRE BELLOC

Where did you come from, baby dear?
Out of the everywhere into here.

GEORGE MACDONALD

Of similarity there's lots
'Twixt tiny tots and Hottentots.

OGDEN NASH

Children are different—mentally, physically, spiritually, quantitatively, qualitatively; and, furthermore, they're all a little bit nuts.

JEAN KERR

Children don't read to find their identity. . . . They still believe in good, the family, angels, devils, witches, goblins, logic, clarity, punctuation and other such obsolete stuff.

ISAAC BASHEVIS SINGER

Father asked us what was God's noblest work. Anna said *men*, but I said *babies*. Men are often bad; babies never are.

LOUISA MAY ALCOTT

Which is the way to Baby-land?
  Any one can tell;
    Up one flight,
    To your right;
Please to ring the bell.

GEORGE COOPER

There is only one pretty child in the world, and every mother has it.

PROVERB

By all published facts in the case,
Children belong to the human race.

Equipped with consciousness, passions, pulse,
They even grow up and become adults.

So why's the resemblance, moral or mental,
Of children to people so coincidental?

PHYLLIS MCGINLEY

Few parents nowadays pay any regard to what their children say to them. The old-fashioned respect for the young is fast dying.

OSCAR WILDE

In your standard-issue family—of which few remain, but on which our expectations are still based—there are parents and there are children. The way you know which are which, aside from certain size and age differences and despite any behavior similarities, is that the parents are the bossy ones.

DELIA EPHRON

Thou shalt not belittle your child.

FITZHUGH DODSON

Parents are the last people on earth who ought to have children.

SAMUEL BUTLER

Now from the coasts of morning pale
Comes safe to port thy tiny sail.
Now have we seen by early sun
Thy miracle of life begun.

GRACE HAZARD CONKLING

Don't forget that compared to a grownup person every baby is a genius. Think of the capacity to learn! The freshness, the temperament, the will of a baby a few months old!

MAY SARTON

Loveliness beyond completeness,
Sweetness distancing all sweetness,
Beauty all that beauty may be—
That's May Bennett, that's my baby.

WILLIAM COX BENNETT

What the mother sings to the cradle goes all the way down to the grave.

HENRY WARD BEECHER

When I was One,
I had just begun.

A. A. MILNE

The character and history of each child may be a new and poetic experience to the parent, if he will let it.

MARGARET FULLER

O dearest, dearest boy! my heart
For better lore would seldom yearn,
Could I but teach the hundredth part
Of what from thee I learn.

WILLIAM WORDSWORTH

If I were asked what single qualification was necessary for one who has the care of children, I should say patience—patience with their tempers, with their understandings, with their progress.

FRANCIS FENELON

Everything is dear to its parent.

SOPHOCLES

[Miss Manners has] been known to make deals with babies, such as "Give me five more minutes' sleep, just five minutes, and I promise you that I'll pick you up and bounce you around again," even though her experience with babies' integrity about fulfilling their sides of bargains has been disillusioning.

JUDITH MARTIN (MISS MANNERS)

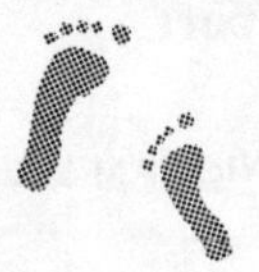

While admitting that adults frequently make unfortunate remarks to babies, it has to be said that babies, too, can make mistakes.

JEAN KERR

A little curly-headed, good-for-nothing,
And mischief-making monkey from his birth.

LORD BYRON

My children always had an unusual diet. . . . In general, they refused to eat anything that hadn't danced on TV.

ERMA BOMBECK

A food is not necessarily essential just because your child hates it.

KATHERINE WHITEHORN

The child's food is mashed, smashed, squashed, ground, filtered, homogenized, served on dishes shaped like windmills, turtles, bears, imprinted with nursery rhymes and puzzles. Children's food must crackle, pop, whistle, talk, sing, and be eaten with itsy-bitsy spoons in itsy-bitsy portions.

SAM LEVENSON

Cooked Carrots: On way to mouth, drop in lap. Smuggle to garbage in napkin.

DELIA EPHRON

My daughter has me totally wrapped around her little finger. I don't even try to win anymore. I just try and save face. I say things to her like, "Go to your room at your earliest convenience. OK. Daddy's going to count to fifteen hundred."

JONATHAN KATZ

Parents learn a lot from their children about coping with life.

MURIEL SPARK

'Most all the time, the whole year round, there ain't
  no flies on me,
But jest 'fore Christmas I'm as good as I kin be!

EUGENE FIELD

Fathers should neither be seen nor heard. That is the only proper basis for family life.

OSCAR WILDE

Every time that I'm your herder
You think you get away with murder.
All right, infant, so you do,
But only because I want you to.

OGDEN NASH

Cortes on his lonely peak in Darien was a pigmy discoverer beside the child eating his first spoonful of ice cream.

HEYWOOD BROUN

It's an interesting fact that babies who won't smile for love or money will smile for vegetables. And the messier the vegetable the more they will smile.

JEAN KERR

Literature is mostly about having sex and not much about having children. Life is the other way round.

DAVID LODGE

To bring up a child in the way he should go, travel that way yourself once in a while.

JOSH BILLINGS

Having at last had one child, we found it no trouble at all to have another. Apparently we had got the combination. I don't know what we did differently, but there must be a little trick to it. It's like riding a bicycle. Once you learn how, you never forget.

RICHARD ARMOUR

I guess the real reason that my wife and I had children is the same reason that Napoleon had for invading Russia: it seemed like a good idea at the time.

BILL COSBY

My son favored the Dwight Eisenhower style so popular with babies, consisting of approximately eight wisps of hair occasionally festooned with creamed spinach.

DAVE BARRY

Our children are not individuals whose rights and tastes are casually respected from infancy, as they are in some primitive societies. . . . They are fundamentally extensions of our own egos and give a special opportunity for the display of authority.

RUTH BENEDICT

Lacking all sense of right and wrong, a child can do nothing which is morally evil, or which merits either punishment or reproof.

JEAN-JACQUES ROUSSEAU

If there is anything that we wish to change in the child, we should first examine it and see whether it is not something that could better be changed in ourselves.

CARL JUNG

It is a shameful thing to insult a little child. It has its feelings, it has its small dignity; and since it cannot defend them, it is surely an ignoble act to injure them.

MARK TWAIN

The best-brought-up children are those who have seen their parents as they are. Hypocrisy is not the parent's first duty.

GEORGE BERNARD SHAW

Permissiveness is the principle of treating children as if they were adults; and the tactic of making sure they never reach that stage.

THOMAS SZASZ

In America there are two classes of travel—first class, and with children.

ROBERT BENCHLEY

And that's the wonderful thing about family travel: it provides you with experiences that will remain locked forever in the scar tissue of your mind.

DAVE BARRY

On the whole, having traveled with children of all the popular ages, I would be inclined to award the Hair-Shirt to the man who successfully completes the ride with a boy of, let us say, three.

ROBERT BENCHLEY

We are always too busy for our children; we never give them the time or interest they deserve. We lavish gifts upon them; but the most precious gift—our personal association, which means so much to them—we give grudgingly.

MARK TWAIN

Children are the true connoisseurs. What's precious to them has no price—only value.

BEL KAUFMAN

Respect the child. Be not too much his parent. Trespass not on his solitude.

RALPH WALDO EMERSON

Your children need your presence more than your presents.

JESSE JACKSON

If men do not keep on speaking terms with children, they cease to be men, and become merely machines for eating and earning money.

JOHN UPDIKE

Parentage is a very important profession, but no test of fitness for it is ever imposed in the interest of the children.

GEORGE BERNARD SHAW

About the only thing we have left that actually discriminates in favor o' the plain people is the stork.

KIN HUBBARD

. . . What in hell
have i done to deserve
all these kittens
i look back on my life
and it seems to me to be
just one damned kitten
after another

DON MARQUIS

Simply having children does not make mothers.

JOHN A. SHEDD

Eat no green apples or you'll droop,
Be careful not to get the croup,
Avoid the chicken-pox and such,
And don't fall out of windows much.

EDWARD ANTHONY

At every step the child should be allowed to meet the real experiences of life; the thorns should never be plucked from his roses.

ELLEN KEY

Never help a child with a task at which he feels he can succeed.

MARIA MONTESSORI

You cannot teach a child to take care of himself unless you will let him try to take care of himself. He will make mistakes; and out of these mistakes will come his wisdom.

HENRY WARD BEECHER

Children do not really need money. After all, they don't have to pay rent or send mailgrams.

FRAN LEBOWITZ

Children should have regular pocket-money, and not be thrown on the world with no practice in fending for themselves out of an earned income.

GEORGE BERNARD SHAW

Designer clothes worn by children are like snowsuits worn by adults. Few can carry it off successfully.

FRAN LEBOWITZ

One should, I think, always give children money, for they will spend it for themselves far more profitably than we can ever spend it for them.

ROSE MACAULAY

The child had every toy his father wanted.

ROBERT E. WHITTEN

What maintains one Vice would bring up two children.

BENJAMIN FRANKLIN

When I bring you coloured toys, my child, I understand why there is such a play of colours on clouds, on water, and why flowers are painted in tints.

RABINDRANATH TAGORE

I have not forgotten how I used to take a child every year to the sea, as to a maternal element better fitted than I to teach, ripen, and perfect the mind and body that I had merely rough-hewn.

COLETTE

Any subject can be taught effectively in some intellectually honest form to any child at any stage of development.

JEROME S. BRUNER

Children do not give up their innate imagination, curiosity, dreaminess easily. You have to love them to get them to do that.

R. D. LAING

A truly appreciative child will break, lose, spoil, or fondle to death any really successful gift within a matter of minutes.

RUSSELL LYNES

No sweeter thing than children's ways and wiles,
  Surely, we say, can gladden eyes and ears
Yet sometimes sweeter than their words or smiles
  Are even their tears.

ALGERNON SWINBURNE

The ability to forget a sorrow is childhood's most enchanting feature.

PHYLLIS MCGINLEY

A child is fed with milk and praise.

MARY LAMB

A child develops individuality long before he develops taste. I have seen my kid straggle into the kitchen in the morning with outfits that need only one accessory: an empty gin bottle.

ERMA BOMBECK

Babies haven't any hair;
Old men's heads are just as bare;
Between the cradle and the grave
Lies a haircut and a shave.

SAMUEL HOFFENSTEIN

Our children are here to stay, but our babies and toddlers and preschoolers are gone as fast as they can grow up—and we have only a short moment with each. When you see a grandfather take a baby in his arms, you see that the moment hasn't always been long enough.

ST. CLAIR ADAMS SULLIVAN

A Child thinks 20 Shillings and 20 Years can scarce ever be spent.

BENJAMIN FRANKLIN

You can leave a bad marriage, a bad job, and a city where the sun never shines. But children are forever.

LEWIS GRIZZARD

Parents lend children their experience and a vicarious memory; children endow their parents with a vicarious immortality.

GEORGE SANTAYANA

We always believe those who resemble us to be beautiful, well-proportioned and, above all, delightful.

JEAN DE LA FONTAINE

I discovered when I had a child of my own that I had become a biased observer of small children. Instead of looking at them with affectionate but nonpartisan eyes, I saw each of them as older or younger, bigger or smaller, more or less graceful, intelligent, or skilled than my own child.

MARGARET MEAD

Nature kindly warps our judgment about our children, especially when they are young, when it would be a fatal thing for them if we did not love them.

GEORGE SANTAYANA

No fathers or mothers think their children ugly.

CERVANTES

If you are a professional, you have probably learned to divide all people into two groups: those whom you want something from and those who want something from you. Children are definitely in the latter group. In fact, they want it all—your love, your attention, and your money.

ALICE KAHN

Children are completely egotistic; they feel their needs intensely and strive ruthlessly to satisfy them.

SIGMUND FREUD

In his youth, everybody believes that the world began to exist only when he was born, and that everything really exists only for his sake.

JOHANN WOLFGANG VON GOETHE

Come along, everybody, see the pretty baby,
Such a pretty baby ought to be adored.
Come along, everybody, come and bore the baby,
See the pretty baby, begging to be bored.

OGDEN NASH

Baby's brain is tired of thinking
On the Wherefore and the Whence;
Baby's precious eyes are blinking
With incipient somnolence.

JAMES JEFFREY ROCHE

Tender are a mother's dreams,
But her babe's not what he seems.
See him plotting in his mind
To grow up some other kind.

CLARENCE DAY

The worst feature of a new baby is its mother's singing.

KIN HUBBARD

Babies do not belong at work or at adult social events. It is no pleasure to them to go to such things, as they are rarely interested in picking up financial tips or salacious gossip and have difficulty reading the subtitles on foreign movies.

JUDITH MARTIN (MISS MANNERS)

We begin life with loss. We are cast from the womb without an apartment, a charge plate, a job or a car.

JUDITH VIORST

If parents would only realize how they bore their children.

GEORGE BERNARD SHAW

It sometimes happens, even in the best of families, that a baby is born. This is not necessarily cause for alarm. The important thing is to keep your wits about you and borrow some money.

ELINOR GOULDING SMITH

Except that right side up is best, there is not much to learn about holding a baby. There are 152 distinctly different ways—and all are right! At least all will do.

HEYWOOD BROUN

A bit of talcum
Is always walcum.

OGDEN NASH

I once knew a chap who had a system of just hanging the baby on the clothes line to dry and he was greatly admired by his fellow citizens for having discovered a wonderful innovation on changing a diaper.

DAMON RUNYON

A child should always say what's true
And speak when he is spoken to,
And behave mannerly at table;
At least as far as he is able.

ROBERT LOUIS STEVENSON

Let thy child's first lesson be obedience, and the second will be what thou wilt.

BENJAMIN FRANKLIN

If you want to discipline a child, instead of doing something simple like training killer bees, you will find that many things are against you, one of which is the child.

BILL COSBY

I've always blamed my shortcomings as a mother on the fact that I studied Child Psychology and Discipline under an unmarried professor whose only experience was in raising a dog. He obviously saw little difference.

ERMA BOMBECK

Fathers, I think, are most apt to appreciate the excellence and attainments of their daughters; mothers, those of their sons.

MENANDER

The boy is the most powerful of all the Hellenes; for the Hellenes are commanded by the Athenians, the Athenians by myself, myself by the boy's mother, and the mother by her boy.

THEMISTOCLES

Of course, I don't always enjoy being a mother. At those times my husband and I hole up somewhere in the wine country, eat, drink, make mad love and pretend we were born sterile and raise poodles.

DOROTHY DEBOLT

Little girls are the nicest things that happen to people. They are born with a little bit of angelshine about them, and though it wears thin sometimes there is always enough left to lasso your heart—even when they are sitting in the mud, or crying temperamental tears, or parading up the street in mother's best clothes.

ALAN BECK

If evolution really works, how come mothers still have only two hands?

ED DUSSAULT

The doll is one of the most imperious necessities, and at the same time one of the most charming instincts of female childhood.

VICTOR HUGO

The real menace in dealing with a five-year-old is that in no time at all you begin to sound like a five-year-old.

JEAN KERR

Nature makes boys and girls lovely to look upon so they can be tolerated until they acquire some sense.

WILLIAM LYON PHELPS

Boys are found everywhere—on top of, underneath, inside of, climbing on, swinging from, running around or jumping to. Mothers love them, little girls hate them, older sisters and brothers tolerate them, adults ignore them and Heaven protects them. A boy is Truth with dirt on its face, Beauty with a cut on its finger, Wisdom with bubble gum in its hair and the Hope of the future with a frog in its pocket.

ALAN BECK

What are little boys made of?
Snips and snails, and puppy dogs' tails;
That's what little boys are made of.

ANONYMOUS

The parent who could see his boy as he really is, would shake his head and say, "Willie is no good; I'll sell him."

STEPHEN BUTLER LEACOCK

I woke before the morning, I was happy all the day,
I never said an ugly word, but smiled and stuck to play.

ROBERT LOUIS STEVENSON

Children do not play ordinary conventional games unless they are encouraged to do so by the older boys and girls. Children's "games," strictly speaking, are not games at all. They are the child's inmost reality! They are the child's life-illusion. They turn back to them with a sigh of relief from the impertinent intrusive activities of grown-up people.

F. C. POWYS

By sports like these are all their cares beguil'd,
The sports of children satisfy the child.

OLIVER GOLDSMITH

Feel the dignity of a child. Do not feel superior to him, for you are not.

ROBERT HENRI

The notion that parents are entitled to respect simply because they are parents is preposterous. The stream of obligation runs strongly the other way. A child owes its parents no gratitude whatever for bringing him into the world (as Swift sardonically said, while they were thinking of something else).

JOHN MACY

To become a father is not hard,
To be a father is, however.

WILHELM BUSCH

By the way, many people make the false assumption that because a baby can't speak he can't hear. As a result, when confronted with an infant, any infant, they raise their voices and speak very distinctly, as though they were ordering a meal in a foreign language.

JEAN KERR

One of the most obvious facts about grown-ups, to a child, is that they have forgotten what it is like to be a child.

RANDALL JARRELL

Give a little love to a child, and you get a great deal back.

JOHN RUSKIN

Children divine those who love them; it is a gift of nature which we lose as we grow up.

PAUL DE KOCK

For the first two years of a child's life you try to get him to talk. For the next ten years you devote your life to getting him to shut up.

ERMA BOMBECK

When I was born, I was so surprised I couldn't talk for a year and a half.

GRACIE ALLEN

There are so many disciplines in being a parent besides the obvious ones like getting up in the night and putting up with the noise during the day. And almost the hardest of all is learning to be a well of affection and not a fountain, to show them we love them, not when *we* feel like it, but when they do.

NAN FAIRBROTHER

It's this way with children. It's cumulative. The more you love them, the more you sacrifice; and the more you sacrifice, the more you love.

WILLIAM GRAHAM SUMNER

Item: And first, I give to good fathers and mothers, but in trust for their children, nevertheless, all good little words of praise and all quaint pet names, and I charge said parents to use them justly, but generously, as the needs of their children shall require.

Item: I leave to children exclusively, but only for the life of their childhood, all and every the dandelions of the fields and the daisies thereof, with the right to play among them freely, according to the custom of children, warning them at the same time against thistles. And I devise to children the yellow shores of creeks and the golden sands beneath the waters thereof, with the dragon-flies that skim the surface of said waters, and the odors of the willows that dip into said waters, and

the white clouds that float high over the giant trees.

And I leave to children the long, long days to be merry in, in a thousand ways, and the Night and the Moon and the train of the Milky Way to wonder at . . .; and I give to each child the right to choose a star that shall be his, and I direct that the child's father shall tell him the name of it, in order that the child shall always remember the name of that star after he has learned and forgotten astronomy.

WILLISTON FISH

Childhood and genius have the same master-organ in common—inquisitiveness.

EDWARD BULWER-LYTTON

There is always one moment in childhood when the door opens and lets the future in.

GRAHAM GREENE

It's a big moment, greater than Balboa seeing the Pacific for the first time, when a baby finds out that those wiggly things on the ends of his arms can be useful in picking up all kinds of interesting objects, and that the ones on the ends of his legs can have other uses besides putting them in his mouth—standing on them, for example.

ART LINKLETTER

A baby is an angel whose wings decrease as his legs increase.

PROVERB

The illusions of childhood are necessary experiences: a child should not be denied a balloon because an adult knows that sooner or later it will burst.

MARCELENE COX

A sweet child is the sweetest thing in nature.

CHARLES LAMB

If there were no children on this earth, there would be no beauty here.

REJEAN DUCHARME

I was fairly sure the baby would be born, but thought it might have three arms or no ears or some other deformity. I had heard that a child might be born misshapen because of the sins of its parents, and while I had not actually done anything bad, I had had some pretty evil thoughts, especially when I was in high school. It was with considerable relief then that when the baby arrived I heard the doctor pronounce it normal.

RICHARD ARMOUR

Babies are necessary to grown-ups. A new baby is like the beginning of all things—wonder, hope, a dream of possibilities.

EDA LESHAN

Of all nature's gifts to the human race, what is sweeter to a man than his children?

CICERO

Children, like dogs, have so sharp a scent that they detect everything—the bad before all the rest.

JOHANN WOLFGANG VON GOETHE

You are the bows from which your children are as living arrows sent forth.

KAHLIL GIBRAN

I believe the power of observation in numbers of very young children to be quite wonderful for its closeness and accuracy.

CHARLES DICKENS

The truth is children are not half-men and half-women, or half-boys and half-girls. They are a race of beings to themselves. And it is in the power of this curious race of beings to plunge into the secret of life more deeply than all other mortals.

J. C. POWYS

Children are made of eyes and ears, and nothing, however minute, escapes their microscopic observation.

FANNY KEMBLE

What children expect from grown-ups is not to be "understood," but only to be loved, even though this love may be expressed clumsily or in sternness. Intimacy does not exist between generations—only trust.

CARL ZUCKER

We can't form our children on our own concepts; we must take them and love them as God gives them to us.

JOHANN WOLFGANG VON GOETHE

I do not love him because he is good, but because he is my little child.

RABINDRANATH TAGORE

Better to be driven out from among men than to be disliked of children.

R. H. DANA

Your responsibility as a parent is not as great as you might imagine. You need not supply the world with the next conqueror of disease or major motion-picture star.

FRAN LEBOWITZ

Children are supposed to help hold a marriage together. They do this in a number of ways. For instance, they demand so much attention that a husband and wife, concentrating on their children, fail to notice each other's faults.

RICHARD ARMOUR

The virtues of mothers shall occasionally be visited upon the children, as well as the sins of the fathers.

CHARLES DICKENS

Every baby born into the world is a finer one than the last.

CHARLES DICKENS

Men love their children, not because they are promising plants, but because they are theirs.

LORD HALIFAX

He is so little to be so large!
Why, a train of cars, or a whale-back barge
Couldn't carry the freight
Of the monstrous weight
Of all his qualities, good and great.
And tho' one view is as good as another,
Don't take my word for it. Ask his mother!

EDMUND VANCE COOKE

Motherhood is the second oldest profession in the world. . . . It's the biggest on-the-job training program in existence today.

ERMA BOMBECK

Some wonder that children should be given to young mothers. But what instruction does the babe bring to the mother. She learns patience, self-control, endurance.

T. W. HIGGINSON

Who of us is mature enough for offspring before the offspring themselves arrive? The value of marriage is not that adults produce children but that children produce adults.

PETER DE VRIES

Fresh air and liberty are all that is necessary to the happiness of children.

THOMAS LOVE PEACOCK

We like little children because they tear out as soon as they get what they want.

KIN HUBBARD

Children don't walk like people. . . . They canter, they bounce, they slither, slide, crawl, leap into the air, saunter, stand on their heads, swing from branch to branch, limp like cripples, or trot like ostriches. But I seldom recall seeing a child just plain walk. They can, however, dawdle.

PHYLLIS MCGINLEY

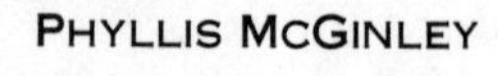

Love is the chain whereby to bind a child to his parents.

ABRAHAM LINCOLN

The quickest way for a parent to get a child's attention is to sit down and look comfortable.

LANE OLINGHOUSE

Whether the father is trying to shave or nap or work, small children come to him like moths to a flame.

BILL COSBY

Cleaning your house while your kids are still growing
Is like shoveling the walk before it stops snowing.

PHYLLIS DILLER

The wildest colts make the best horses.

PLUTARCH

There is no such thing as fun for the whole family.

JERRY SEINFELD

Your children are not your children.
They are the sons and daughters of Life's longing for itself.

KAHLIL GIBRAN

It is not just Mowgli who was raised by a couple of wolves; any child is raised by a couple of grown-ups. Father and Mother may be nearer and dearer than anyone will ever be again—still, they are members of a different species.

RANDALL JARRELL

We think our children a part of ourselves, though as they grow up they might very well undeceive us.

LORD HALIFAX

In order to influence a child, one must be careful not to be that child's parent or grandparent.

DON MARQUIS

Little children are still the symbol of the eternal marriage between love and duty.

GEORGE ELIOT

If one day you have the children that we want you to have, you'll discover exactly where gray hairs come from.

SIDNEY POITIER

I believe that all women, but especially housewives, tend to think in lists. . . . The idea of a series of items, following one another docilely, forms the only possible reasonable approach to life if you have to live it with a home and a husband and children, none of whom would dream of following one another docilely.

SHIRLEY JACKSON

One moment makes a father, but a mother
Is made by endless moments, load on load.

JOHN G. NEIHARDT

I love these little people; and it is not a slight thing when they, who are so fresh from God, love us.

CHARLES DICKENS

He that has no children knows not what is love.

PROVERB

Children should realize that parents are emotionally insecure, and that there are times when they need loving kindness. Unfortunately, a relationship with a child, like any love affair, is complicated by the fact that the two parties almost never feel the same amount of ardor at the same time.

JEAN KERR

Grown-ups never understand anything for themselves, and it is tiresome for children to be always and forever explaining things to them.

ANTOINE DE SAINT-EXUPERY

Is not a young mother one of the sweetest sights life shows us?

WILLIAM MAKEPEACE THACKERAY

The idea with natural childbirth is to avoid drugs so the mother can share the first intimate moments after birth with the baby and the father and the obstetrician and the standby anesthesiologist and the nurses and the person who cleans the room.

DAVE BARRY

If Nature had arranged that husbands and wives should have children alternatively, there would never be more than *three* in a family.

LAURENCE HOUSMAN

Do not videotape your child in the bathtub. Do not name your child after a Scandinavian deity or any aspect of the weather.

DANIEL MENAKER

The simplest toy, one which even the youngest child can operate, is called a grandparent.

SAM LEVENSON

A mother's hardest to forgive.
Life is the fruit she longs to hand you,
Ripe on a plate. And while you live,
Relentlessly she understands you.

PHYLLIS MCGINLEY

There are only two things a child will share willingly—communicable diseases and his mother's age.

DR. BENJAMIN SPOCK

Another thing that Daddy ain't,
I frankly tell you, is a saint.

OGDEN NASH

No one ever keeps a secret so well as a child.

VICTOR HUGO

You can do anything with children if you only play with them.

OTTO VON BISMARCK

Children are entitled to their otherness, as anyone is; and when we reach them, as we sometimes do, it is generally on a point of sheer delight, to us so astonishing, but to them so natural.

ALASTAIR REID

If a child is to keep alive his inborn sense of wonder, he needs the companionship of at least one adult who can share it, rediscovering with him the joy, excitement and mystery of the world we live in.

RACHEL CARSON

Some of my best friends are children. In fact, all of my best friends are children.

J. D. SALINGER

Monday's child is fair of face,
Tuesday's child is full of grace,
Wednesday's child is full of woe,
Thursday's child has far to go,
Friday's child is loving and giving,
Saturday's child has to work for its living,
But a child that's born on the Sabbath day
Is fair and wise and good and gay.

ANONYMOUS

No one knows what will be the fate of the child he begets, or the child she bears. The fate of the child is the last thing they consider.

CLARENCE DARROW

If children grew up according to early indications, we should have nothing but geniuses.

JOHANN WOLFGANG VON GOETHE

How do you like to go up in a swing,
Up in the air so blue?
Oh, I do think it the pleasantest thing
Ever a child can do!

ROBERT LOUIS STEVENSON

Never fear spoiling children by making them too happy. Happiness is the atmosphere in which all good affections grow.

ANN BRAY

Children think not of what is past nor what is to come; they enjoy the present, which very few of us do.

JEAN DE LA BRUYERE

Beware of making childhood's griefs your own. They are no more lasting than soap bubbles.

PHYLLIS MCGINLEY

Children are extremely cruel without intending it; and in ninety-nine cases out of a hundred the reason is that they do not conceive their elders as having any human feelings. Serve the elders right, perhaps, for posing as superhuman!

GEORGE BERNARD SHAW

There should be no enforced respect for grown-ups. We cannot prevent children from thinking us fools by merely forbidding them to utter their thoughts.

BERTRAND RUSSELL

"But he hasn't got anything on," a little child said.

HANS CHRISTIAN ANDERSEN

Anything which parents have not learned from experience they can now learn from their children.

ANONYMOUS

The intrinsic charm and goodness of childhood still constitute the best guarantee of the further perfectibility of mankind.

DR. ARNOLD GESELL

When the voices of children are heard on the green
And laughing is heard on the hill,
My heart is at rest within my breast
And everything else is still.

WILLIAM BLAKE

Like father, like son: every good tree maketh good fruits.

WILLIAM LANGLAND

The greatest poem ever known
Is one all poets have outgrown:
The poetry, innate, untold,
Of being only four years old.

CHRISTOPHER MORLEY

So both the Raven and the Ape think their own young the fairest.

SIR THOMAS MORE

All God's children are not beautiful. Most of God's children are, in fact, barely presentable.

FRAN LEBOWITZ

A soiled baby, with a neglected nose, cannot be conscientiously regarded as a thing of beauty.

MARK TWAIN

Childhood, n. The period of human life intermediate between the idiocy of infancy and the folly of youth—two removes from the sin of manhood and three from the remorse of age.

AMBROSE BIERCE

Youth is a wonderful thing. What a crime to waste it on children.

GEORGE BERNARD SHAW

You can imagine how shocked Miss Manners was to hear where babies come from. Babies, it seems, no longer appear from vegetable gardens or express deliveries by large birds (who refuse to leave them if you're not home to sign for them, even though they never tell you exactly when they will arrive).

JUDITH MARTIN (MISS MANNERS)

How beautifully everything is arranged by Nature; as soon as a child enters the world, it finds a mother ready to take care of it.

JULES MICHELET

Children and fools cannot lie.

JOHN HEYWOOD

Teach your child to hold his tongue, he'll learn fast enough to speak.

BENJAMIN FRANKLIN

The little girl had the making of a poet in her who, being told to be sure of her meaning before she spoke, said, "How can I know what I think till I see what I say?"

GRAHAM WALLAS

A woman who is very anxious to get children always reads *storks* instead of *stocks*.

SIGMUND FREUD

Pretty much all the honest truth telling there is in the world is done by children.

OLIVER WENDELL HOLMES

Insisted on much in my earlier years,
To wit. Little pitchers have very long ears!

RICHARD HARRIS BARHAM

My childhood should have taught me lessons for my own fatherhood, but it didn't because parenting can be learned only by people who have no children.

BILL COSBY

To my embarrassment, I was born in bed with a lady.

WILSON MIZNER

Children will grow up substantially what they *are* by nature—and only that.

HARRIET BEECHER STOWE

It is pretty generally held that all a woman needs to do to know all about children is to have some. This wisdom is attributed to instinct. . . . I have seen mothers give beer and spaghetti and Neapolitan ice cream to children in arms, and if they got that from instinct the only conclusion possible is that instinct is not what it used to be.

HEYWOOD BROUN

When Mrs. Frederick C. Little's second son was born, everybody noticed that he was not much bigger than a mouse. The truth of the matter was, the baby looked very much like a mouse in every way.

E. B. WHITE

From the moment of his birth the customs into which [an individual] is born shape his experience and behavior. By the time he can talk, he is the little creature of his culture.

RUTH BENEDICT

Behold the child, by Nature's kindly law,
Pleas'd with a rattle, tickled with a straw.

ALEXANDER POPE

Who is there whom bright and agreeable children do not attract to play and creep and prattle with them?

EPICTETUS

A mountain in labour shouted so loud that everyone, summoned by the noise, ran up expecting that she would be delivered of a city bigger than Paris; she brought forth a mouse.

JEAN DE LA FONTAINE

Beat upon mine, little heart! beat, beat!
Beat upon mine! you are mine, my sweet!
All mine from your pretty blue eyes to your feet,
My sweet!

ALFRED, LORD TENNYSON

The kind of man who thinks that helping with the dishes is beneath him will also think that helping with the baby is beneath him, and then he certainly is not going to be a very successful father.

ELEANOR ROOSEVELT

I was influenced by my mother. Every man is when he is young.

OSCAR WILDE

The art of never making a mistake is crucial to motherhood. To be effective and to gain the respect she needs to function, a mother must have her children believe she has never engaged in sex, never made a bad decision, never caused her own mother a moment's anxiety, and was never a child.

ERMA BOMBECK

Children begin by loving their parents. After a time they judge them. Rarely, if ever do they forgive them.

OSCAR WILDE

The only thing that seems eternal and natural in motherhood is ambivalence.

JANE LAZARRE

Thy daughters bright thy walks adorn,
Gay as the gilded summer sky,
Sweet as the dewy, milky-white thorn,
Dear as the raptured thrill of joy.

ROBERT BURNS

Children, you are very little,
And your bones are very brittle;
If you would grow great and stately,
You must try to walk sedately.

ROBERT LOUIS STEVENSON

Child, you are like a flower,
So sweet and pure and fair.
I look at you, and sadness
Touches me with a prayer.

HEINRICH HEINE

There was a little girl
Who had a little curl
Right in the middle of her forehead;
And when she was good
She was very, very good,
But when she was bad she was horrid.

HENRY WADSWORTH LONGFELLOW

You have to wonder about a girl's bedroom when you go in to make her bed and her dolls have a look of fear and disbelief in their eyes.

ERMA BOMBECK

A Trick that everyone abhors
In Little Girls is slamming Doors.

HILAIRE BELLOC

I often think it's comical
How nature always does contrive
That every boy and every gal,
That's born into the world alive,
Is either a little Liberal,
Or else a little Conservative!

SIR WILLIAM S. GILBERT

There's no reason why any child should lack a complete knowledge of life, since there is no censorship of drugstore windows.

DON HEROLD

Do not, on a rainy day, ask your child what he feels like doing, because I assure you that what he feels like doing, you won't feel like watching.

FRAN LEBOWITZ

What is a child? An experiment. A fresh attempt to produce the just man made perfect: that is, to make humanity divine.

GEORGE BERNARD SHAW

A baby is God's opinion that the world should go on.

CARL SANDBURG

"I have no name;
I am but two days old."
What shall I call thee?
"I happy am,
Joy is my name."

WILLIAM BLAKE

I'm youth, I'm joy, I'm a little bird that has broken out of the egg.

SIR J. M. BARRIE

Children need love, especially when they do not deserve it.

HAROLD S. HULBERT

Mother Nature, in her infinite wisdom, has instilled within each of us a powerful biological instinct to reproduce; this is her way of assuring that the human race, come what may, will never have any disposable income.

DAVE BARRY

We don't refer to these as commercials, Uncle Edgar. They're just helpful shopping reminders to the boys and girls—and they blend right in with your story.

BOB ELLIOTT AND RAY GOULDING

Babies are unreasonable; they expect far too much of existence. Each new generation that comes takes one look at the world, thinks wildly, "Is *this* all they've done to it?" and bursts into tears.

CLARENCE DAY

Babe or *Baby*, *n.* A misshapen creature of no particular age, sex, or condition, chiefly remarkable for the violence of the sympathies and antipathies it excites in others, itself without sentiment or emotion.

AMBROSE BIERCE

As soon as I stepped out of my mother's womb on to dry land, I realized that I had made a mistake—that I shouldn't have come—but the trouble with children is that they are not returnable.

QUENTIN CRISP

Equality for women demands a change in the human psyche more profound than anything Marx dreamed of. It means valuing parenthood as much as we value banking.

POLLY TOYNBEE

But what's more important. Building a bridge or taking care of a baby?

JUNE JORDAN

The birth of a child erases all previous marital agreements.

SUSAN CHEEVER

The greatest fantasy many pregnant women have during that time when the imagination seems particularly ripe is that of a fairy godmother called childcare.

ALICE KAHN

A father is a banker provided by nature.

ANONYMOUS

Children's talent to endure stems from their ignorance of alternatives.

MAYA ANGELOU

A baby is an inestimable blessing and bother.

MARK TWAIN

Now the thing about having a baby—and I can't be the first person to have noticed this—is that thereafter you *have* it, and it's years before you can distract it from any elemental need by saying, "Oh, for heaven's sake, go look at television."

JEAN KERR

Being constantly with children was like wearing a pair of shoes that were expensive and too small. She couldn't bear to throw them out, but they gave her blisters.

BERYL BAINBRIDGE

Among the great numbers of people who have volunteered to go to the moon are several thousand young mothers who have offered either themselves or their children.

SAM LEVENSON

Children have more need of models than of critics.

JOSEPH JOUBERT

My father had always said that there are four things a child needs—plenty of love, nourishing food, regular sleep, and lots of soap and water—and after those, what he needs most is some intelligent neglect.

IVY BAKER PRIEST

Water fascinates kids. They run toward it, and they run away from it. They love it in a lake or an ocean, but it's a necessary evil in a bathtub. They'll swim in it, sail on it, dangle feet in it—but fight to keep it away from that sacred area behind their ears.

ART LINKLETTER

Men profess a total lack of ability to wash a baby's face simply because they believe there's no great fun in the business, at either end of the sponge.

HEYWOOD BROUN

It used to be believed that the parent had unlimited claims on the child and rights over him. In a truer view of the matter, we are coming to see that the rights are on the side of the child and the duties on the side of the parent.

WILLIAM GRAHAM SUMNER

Certainly children should obey their fathers. But fathers, also, should not be reluctant to humour their children.

GIAMBATTISTA CINTHIO GIRALDI

He is too experienced a parent ever to make positive promises.

CHRISTOPHER MORLEY

Don't take up a man's time talking about the smartness of your children; he wants to talk to you about the smartness of his children.

E. W. HOWE

I never met anyone who didn't have a very smart child. What happens to these children, you wonder, when they reach adulthood?

FRAN LEBOWITZ

Parents of young children should realize that few people, and maybe no one, will find their children as enchanting as they do.

BARBARA WALTERS

She never quite leaves her children at home, even when she doesn't take them along.

MARGARET CULKIN BANNING

No one has yet fully realized the wealth of sympathy, kindness and generosity hidden in the soul of the child. The effort of every true education should be to unlock that treasure.

EMMA GOLDMAN

The object of teaching a child is to enable him to get along without a teacher.

ELBERT HUBBARD

Never teach your child to be cunning, for you may be certain you will be one of the very first victims of his shrewdness.

JOSH BILLINGS

If you want to see what children can do, you must stop giving them things.

NORMAN DOUGLAS

If you want a baby, have a new one. Don't baby the old one.

JESSAMYN WEST

For what she does not know, she eats,
A worm, a twig, a block, a fly,
And every novel thing she meets
Is bitten into bye and bye.

ROBERT NATHAN

Animal Crackers: Eat each in this order—legs, head, body.

DELIA EPHRON

We love those we feed, not vice versa; in caring for others we nourish our own self-esteem. Children are dependent upon adults. It's a craven role for a child. It's very natural to want to bite the hand that feeds you.

JESSAMYN WEST

Ask your child what he wants for dinner only if he's buying.

FRAN LEBOWITZ

Child, with many a childish wile,
Timid look, and blushing smile,
Downy wings to steal thy way,
Gilded bow, and quiver gay,
Who in thy simple mien would trace
The tyrant of the human race?

JOANNA BAILLIE

I have found the best way to give advice to your children is to find out what they want and then advise them to do it.

HARRY S. TRUMAN

The thing that impresses me most about America is the way parents obey their children.

KING EDWARD VIII (DUKE OF WINDSOR)

Don't set your wit against a child.

JONATHAN SWIFT

I do not believe in a child world. It is a fantasy world. I believe the child should be taught from the very first that the whole world is his world, that adult and child share one world, that all generations are needed.

PEARL BUCK

It is not enough for parents to understand children. They must accord children the privilege of understanding them.

MILTON R. SAPIRSTEIN

There are only two lasting bequests we can hope to give our children. One of these is roots, the other, wings.

HODDING CARTER

If help and salvation are to come, they can only come from the children, for the children are the makers of men.

MARIA MONTESSORI

What is the matter with Mary Jane?
She's crying with all her might and main,
And she won't eat her dinner—rice pudding again—
What *is* the matter with Mary Jane?

A. A. MILNE

Remember, when they have a tantrum, don't have one of your own.

DR. JUDITH KURIANSKY

Incidentally, the worst stage a kid ever goes through is the one he is going through right now.

SAM LEVENSON

I have always admired women who can reach out to pat their children and not have them flinch.

ERMA BOMBECK

If children and adults differ in their approach to bedtime, there is even greater discrepancy in the separate ways they greet the morn.

JEAN KERR

There are, in the maternal catalog, dozens of dazzling virtues. But if I had to choose my favorite from the list—that long list which includes such high and heroic qualities as fortitude, patience, compassion, and self-sacrifice—I would single out a smaller one. I would choose casualness.

PHYLLIS McGINLEY

Begin, baby boy, to recognize your mother by a smile.

VERGIL

Bringing up a family should be an adventure, not an anxious discipline in which everybody is constantly graded for performance.

MILTON R. SAPIRSTEIN

Allow children to be happy their own way: for what better way will they ever find?

DR. SAMUEL JOHNSON

When I became a father, I learned that insanity in children, like radio transmission, is liveliest at night.

BILL COSBY

In point of fact, we are all born rude. No infant has ever appeared yet with the grace to understand how inconsiderate it is to disturb others in the middle of the night.

JUDITH MARTIN (MISS MANNERS)

Adam and Eve had many advantages, but the principal one was that they escaped teething.

MARK TWAIN

A child is like an ax; even if it hurts you, you still carry it on your shoulder.

PROVERB

Sweet babe, in thy face
Soft desires I can trace,
Secret joys and secret smiles,
Little pretty infant wiles.

WILLIAM BLAKE

The infant's instinctive smile seems to have exactly that purpose which is its crowning effect, namely, that the adult feels recognized, and in return expresses recognition in the form of loving and providing.

ERIC ERIKSON

At six weeks Baby grinned a grin
That spread from mouth to eyes to chin,
And Doc, the smartie, had the brass
To tell me it was only gas!

MARGARET FISHBACK

Oh, what a tangled web we weave when first we practice to conceive.

DON HEROLD

Because in the end, the negative aspects of being a parent—the loss of intimacy, the expense, the total lack of free time, the incredible burden of responsibility, the constant nagging fear of having done the wrong thing, etc.—are more than outweighed by the positive aspects, such as never again lacking for primitive drawings to attach to your refrigerator with magnets.

DAVE BARRY

One of the disadvantages of having children is that they eventually get old enough to give you presents they make at school.

ROBERT BYRNE

We all of us wanted babies—but did we want children?

EDA LESHAN

The precursor of the mirror is the mother's face.

D. W. WINNICOTT

Could we understand half what mothers say and do to us when infants we should be filled with such conceit of our own importance as would make us insupportable through life.

AUGUST W. AND JULIUS C. HARE

Who ran to help me when I fell,
And would some pretty story tell,
Or kiss the place to make it well?
My Mother.

ANN AND JANE TAYLOR

Mother is the name for God in the lips and hearts of little children.

WILLIAM MAKEPEACE THACKERAY

Trust not your daughters' minds
By what you see them act.

WILLIAM SHAKESPEARE

A boy is a magical creature—you can lock him out of your workshop, but you can't lock him out of your heart. You can get him out of your study, but you can't get him out of your mind. Might as well give up—he is your captor, your jailer, your boss and your master—a freckled-faced, pint-sized, cat-chasing bundle of noise. But when you come home at night with only the shattered pieces of your hopes and dreams, he can mend them like new with two magic words—"Hi, Dad!"

ALAN BECK

You're a perfect child, a stubborn child! Your mind's in pigtails, like your hair!

MARY ROBERTS RINEHART

A daughter is an embarrassing and ticklish possession.

MENANDER

One of the best things in the world to be is a boy; it requires no experience, but needs some practice to be a good one.

CHARLES DUDLEY WARNER

A ship under sail, a man in complete armour, and a woman with a big belly, are the three handsomest sights in the world.

JAMES HOWELL

A little girl can be sweeter (and badder) oftener than anyone else in the world. She can jitter around, and stomp, and make funny noises that frazzle your nerves, yet just when you open your mouth she stands there demure with that special look in her eyes. A girl is Innocence playing in the mud, Beauty standing on its head, and Motherhood dragging a doll by the foot.

ALAN BECK

Of all the animals, the boy is the most unmanageable.

PLATO

As much as I converse with sages and heroes, they have very little of my love and admiration. I long for rural and domestic scenes, for the warbling of birds and the prattling of my children.

JOHN ADAMS

We received only one pair of booties, and those were a pair of rosebud-covered white ones that someone had sent my first child when he was born and which I had given, still in their original pink tissue paper, to a friend when *her* first child was born. . . . I have them carefully set aside, because I know someone who is having a baby in June.

SHIRLEY JACKSON

Families with babies and families without babies are sorry for each other.

E. W. HOWE

Familiarity breeds contempt—and children.

MARK TWAIN

Children are poor men's riches.

PROVERB

Perhaps a better woman after all,
With chubby children hanging on my neck
To keep me low and wise.

ELIZABETH BARRETT BROWNING

There is no commitment in the world like having children. Even though they often will drive you to consider commitment of another kind, the value of a family still cannot be measured.

BILL COSBY

My wife and I were blessed with two kids and eight hundred theories beamed at us every day, all day, from magazines, radio and TV programs, diaper-service bulletins, books, pamphlets, checklists, progress charts, authorities, authorities, authorities.

SAM LEVENSON

I never understood why babies were created with all the component parts necessary for a rich, full life . . . with the unfinished plumbing left to amateurs. If it was a matter of money, there isn't a mother in this world who wouldn't have chipped in a few extra bucks to have the kid completely assembled, trained, and ready to take on long trips.

ERMA BOMBECK

Training a child is more or less a matter of pot luck.

ROD MACLEAN

One of the most important things to remember about infant care is: never change diapers in mid-stream.

DON MARQUIS

Babies: A loud noise at one end and no sense of responsibility at the other.

FATHER RONALD KNOX

In spite of the six thousand manuals on child raising in the bookstores, child raising is still a dark continent and no one really knows anything.

BILL COSBY

Parenthood remains the greatest single preserve of the amateur.

ALVIN TOFFLER

The finest inheritance you can give to a child is to allow it to make its own way, completely on its own feet.

ISADORA DUNCAN

It is wise to remember that rebellion belongs to the freedom you have given your child by bringing him or her up in such a way that he or she exists in his or her own right. In some instances it could be said: "You sowed a baby and you reaped a bomb." In fact this is always true, but it does not always look like it.

D. W. WINNICOTT

It is not a bad thing that children should occasionally, and politely, put their parents in their place.

COLETTE

Oh, grown-ups cannot understand
  And grown-ups never will,
How short the way to fairyland,
  Across the purple hill.

ALFRED NOYES

The best way to raise a child is to LAY OFF.

SHULAMITH FIRESTONE

The plays of natural lively children are the infancy of art. Children live in the world of imagination and feeling. They invest the most insignificant object with any form they please, and see in it whatever they wish to see.

ADAM G. OEHLENSCHLAGER

A little child, a limber elf,
Singing, dancing to itself,

. . .

Makes such a vision to the sight
As fills a father's eyes with light.

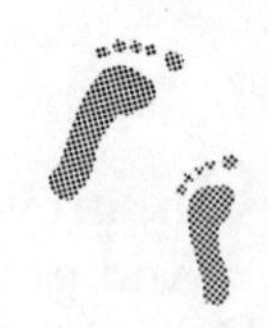

SAMUEL COLERIDGE

There never was a child so lovely but his mother was glad to get him asleep.

RALPH WALDO EMERSON

Wynken, Blynken, and Nod one night
  Sailed off in a wooden shoe—
Sailed on a river of crystal light,
  Into a sea of dew.

. . .

Wynken and Blynken are two little eyes,
  And Nod is a little head,
And the wooden shoe that sailed the skies
  Is a wee one's trundle-bed.

EUGENE FIELD

Baby's bedtime is the twilight zone of sanity in the child-centered home.

SAM LEVENSON

Babies do not want to hear about babies; they like to be told of giants and castles, and of somewhat which can stretch and stimulate their little minds.

DR. SAMUEL JOHNSON

Boys like romantic tales; but babies like realistic tales—because they find them romantic.

G. K. CHESTERTON

Child of the pure, unclouded brow
And dreaming eyes of wonder!
Though time be fleet and I and thou
Are half a life asunder,
Thy loving smile will surely hail
The love-gift of a fairy tale.

LEWIS CARROLL

Children consider one perusal of a book only the aperitif before the meal.

PHYLLIS MCGINLEY

Home—the nursery of the infinite.

WILLIAM ELLERY CHANNING

Know you what it is to be a child? It is to be something very different from the man of today. It is to have a spirit yet streaming from the waters of baptism; it is to believe in love, to believe in loveliness, to believe in belief; it is to be so little that the elves can reach to whisper in your ear; it is to turn pumpkins into coaches, and mice into horses, lowness into loftiness, and nothing into everything, for each child has its fairy godmother in its soul; it is to live in a nutshell and to count yourself the king of infinite space.

FRANCIS THOMSON

You have to ask children and birds how cherries and strawberries taste.

JOHANN WOLFGANG VON GOETHE

When you take baby to church or on the train, be sure to have plenty of cookies and chloroform.

DON HEROLD

It takes about an hour and a half to get the contemporary child dressed to go out and play for eight minutes.

SAM LEVENSON

How delightful when children resemble their parents!

NOSSIS

Children generally hate to be idle.

JOHN LOCKE

What feeling is so nice as a child's hand in yours? So small, so soft and warm, like a kitten huddling in the shelter of your clasp.

MARJORIE HOLMES

My mother taught me my ABCs. From my father I learned the glories of going to the bathroom outside.

LEWIS GRIZZARD

He argued that the principal duty which a parent owed to a child was to make him happy.

ANTHONY TROLLOPE

Yes, Virginia, there is a Santa Claus. . . . Alas! how dreary would be the world if there were no Santa Claus. It would be as dreary as if there were no Virginias. . . . The eternal light with which childhood fills the world would be extinguished.

FRANCIS CHURCH

Before I got married I had six theories about bringing up children; now I have six children, and no theories.

LORD ROCHESTER

We are apt to make the usual blunder of emptying the baby out with the bath.

GEORGE BERNARD SHAW

Young people are always more given to admiring what is gigantic than what is reasonable.

EUGENE DELACROIX

Something you consider bad may bring out your child's talents; something you consider good may stifle them.

CHATEAUBRIAND

There is little use to talk about your child to anyone; other people either have one or haven't.

DON HEROLD

Always end the name of your child with a vowel, so that when you yell, the name will carry.

BILL COSBY

Children are aliens, and we treat them as such.

RALPH WALDO EMERSON

When children appear, we justify all our weaknesses, compromises, snobberies, by saying: "It's for the children's sake."

ANTON CHEKHOV